Wedding Coloring Book

Colors of Abundance Vol. 5

by Julia Stueber

www.colorsofabundance.com

Disclaimer and Copyright Notification:

Copyright © 2016 by Julia Stüber

Julia Stüber
Adalbert-Stifter-Str. 2

53721 Siegburg

Germany

www.colorsofabundance.com
info@colorsofabundance.com

ISBN-13: 978-1533345516
ISBN-10: 1533345511

The contents in this book are based on the author's personal experience and research. Your results may vary, and will be based on your individual situation and motivation. There are no guarantees concerning the level of success you may experience. Your individual success depends on your motivation, dedication, background and desire.

About Julia Stüber:

Born 1973, married and mother, was born in Bonn, Germany, where she studied German literature and language as well as Computational Linguistics. Since 2009 she has been blogging about various nutritional subjects. She is a trained psychological counselor as well as a nutritional coach. For the last 2 years she has been seen creating mandalas or coloring book everywhere she goes. That is why she is now including coloring and drawing mandalas in her life coaching.

You can find out more about her coaching offers here:
www.colorsofabundance.com/coaching

A Welcome & A Thank You

A wedding should be the best day in life, but at the same time it is one of the most stressful. This is where coloring comes in handy for relaxing. You only have to follow one important rule about how to use this book:

There are no rules!

You can start at the beginning and go page after page. Or you choose a page that speaks to you. And of course you can leave out those pages you don't like. The same applies for the images itself. You can start in the middle and work your way away from the center. You can start from right to left, or left to right. Or you first color all the parts you would like to have in one color and then proceed with the next color. It is really up to you!

Which Colors Should You Use?
You can choose pens, crayons, markers, watercolors - whatever colors you have. And you don't have to be realistic in choosing the colors, just choose those that speak to you in this very moment.
As for pens I prefer markers and "Stabilo Cappies" as they have bright colors and the cappies are connected with a band , so I don't loose any of the them while on the go - yes, I have been caught in my favorite coffee shop in town coloring mandalas!

Most important: Have fun!

I hope you will have a wonderful wedding!
Your
Julia Stueber

Please visit my Facebook page for free coloring pages:
http://www.colorsofabundance.com/facebook

Testpage

Please use this page to try your pens and colors
and how they work on this kind of paper!

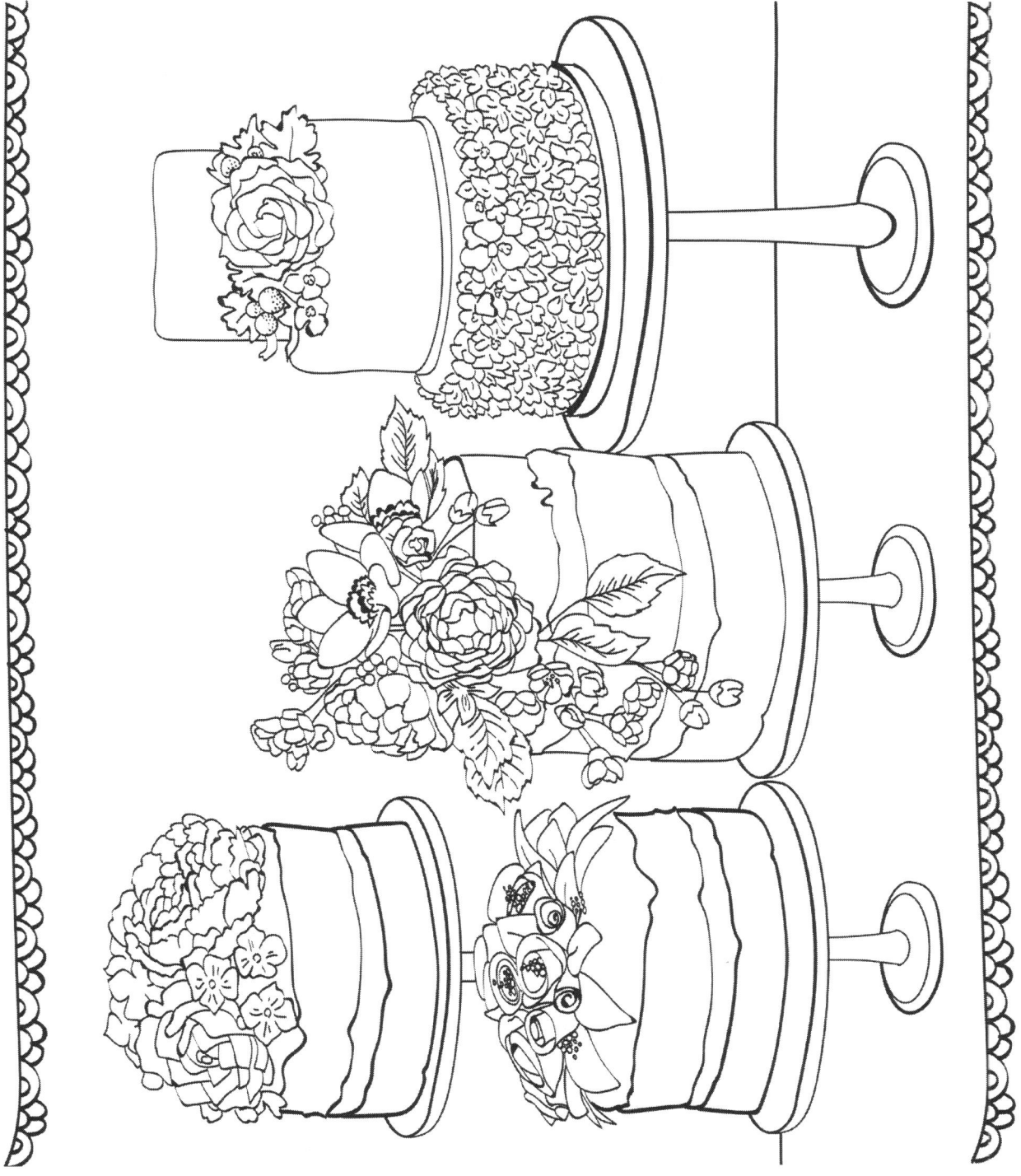

LOVE

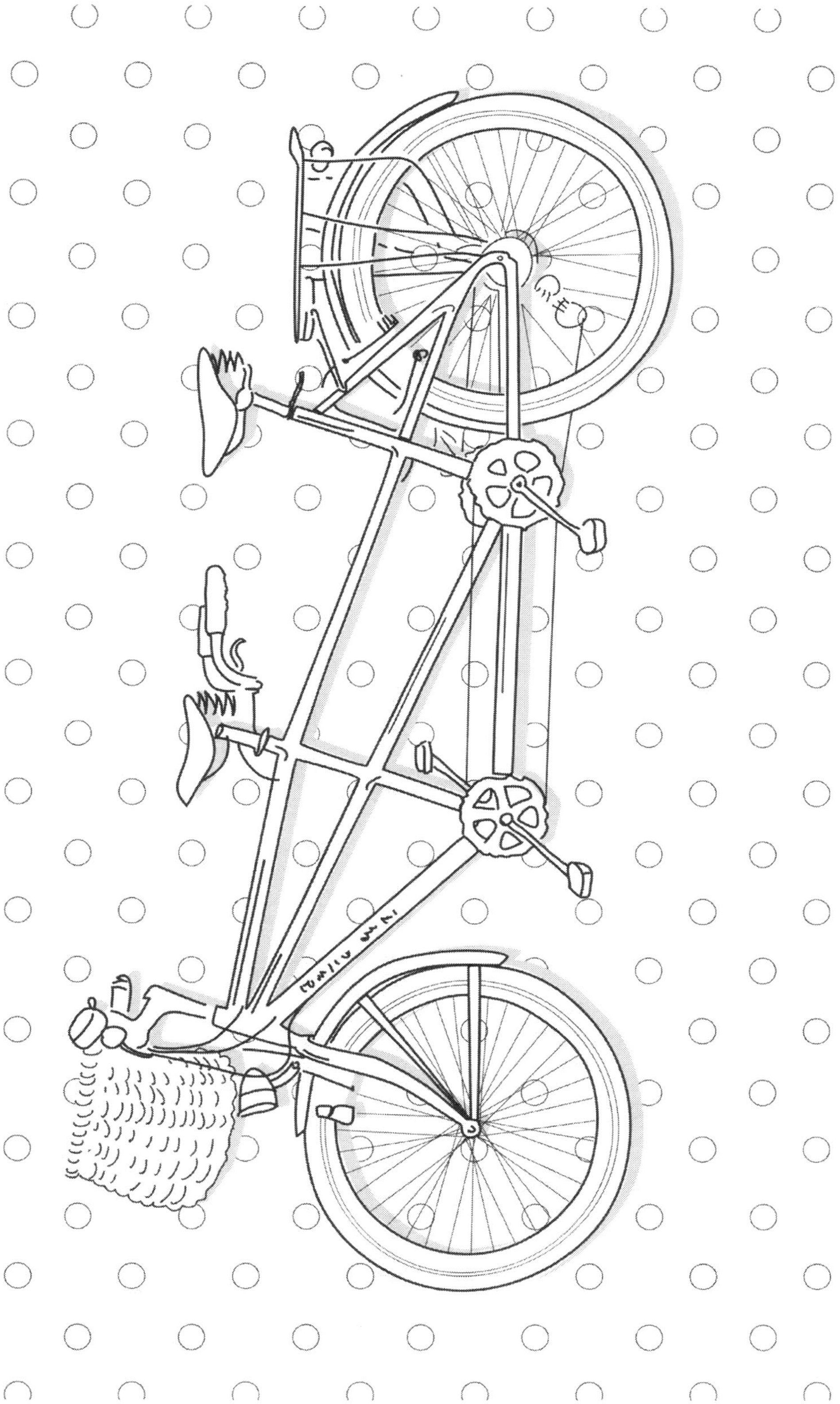

LOVE

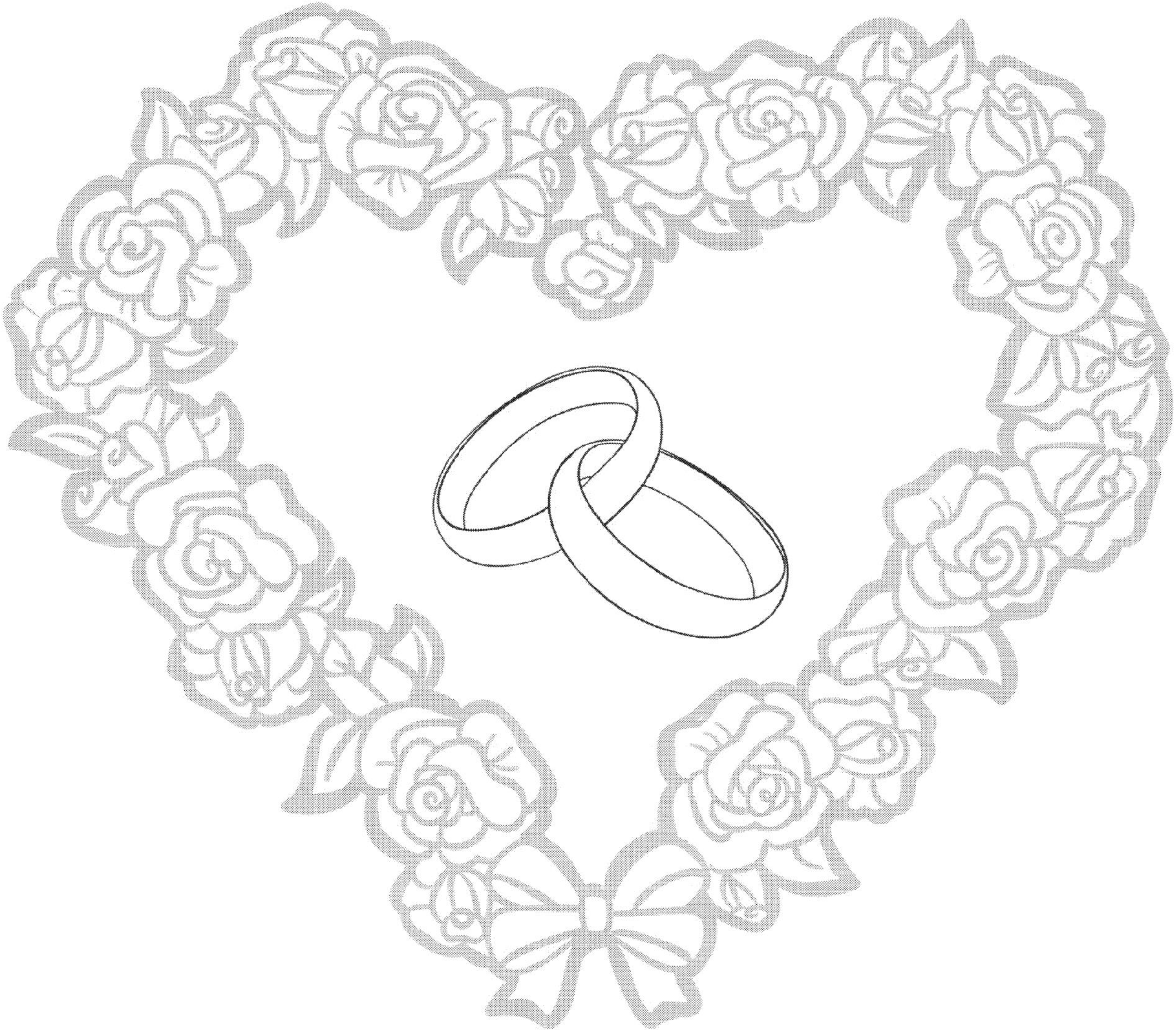

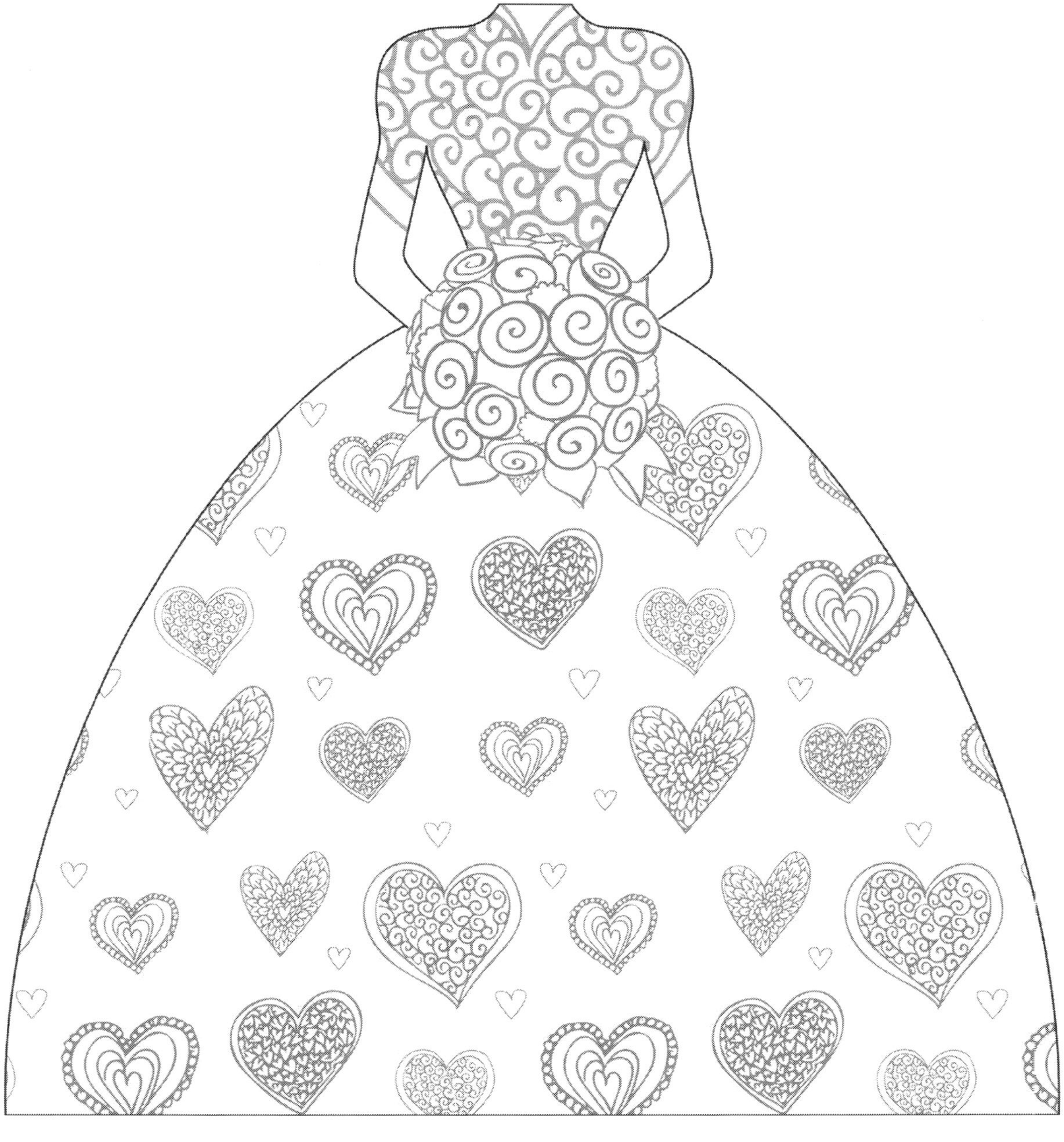

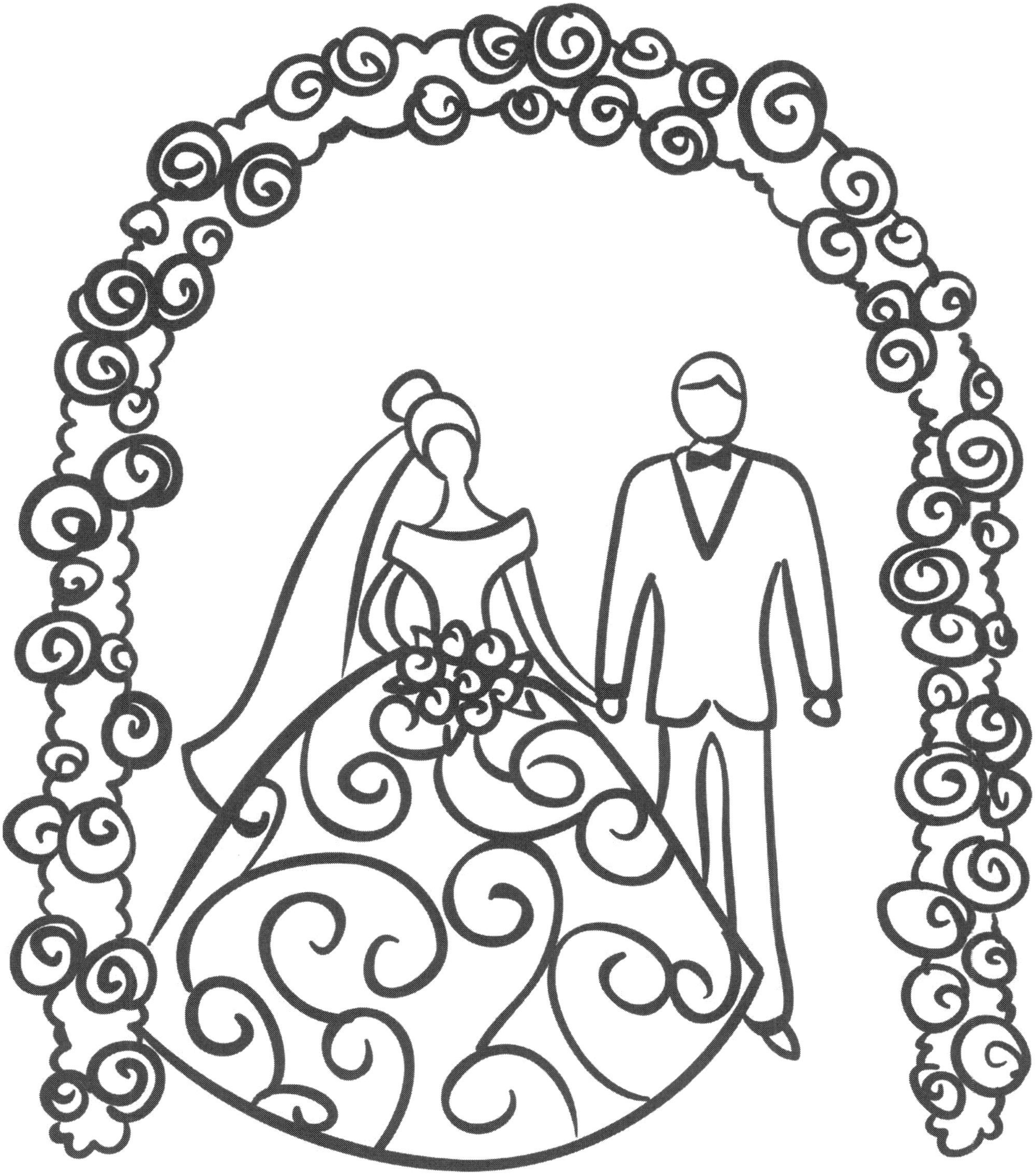

Discover more books from the series „Colors of Abundance"

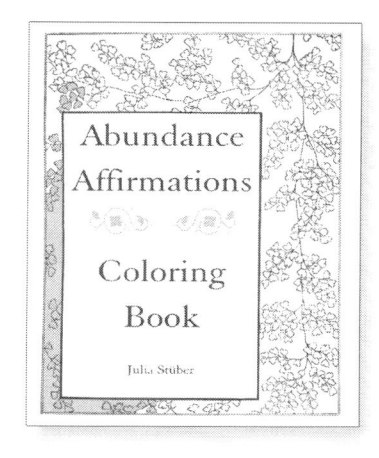

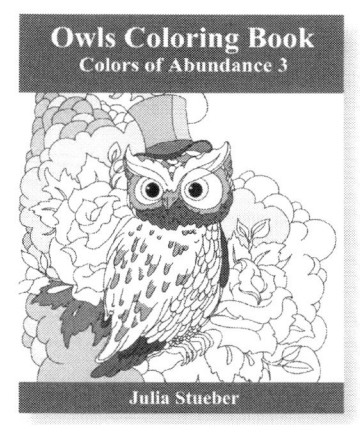

www.colorsofabundance.com/my-books/

Printed in Great Britain
by Amazon